I0410744

I AM BEAUTIFUL...

#YOUAREASTAR

_____

_____

_____

_____

_____

_____

_____

_____

LET'S DOODLE!

GET CREATIVE! LET YOUR IMAGINATION RUN WILD!

#EXPRESSYOURSELF

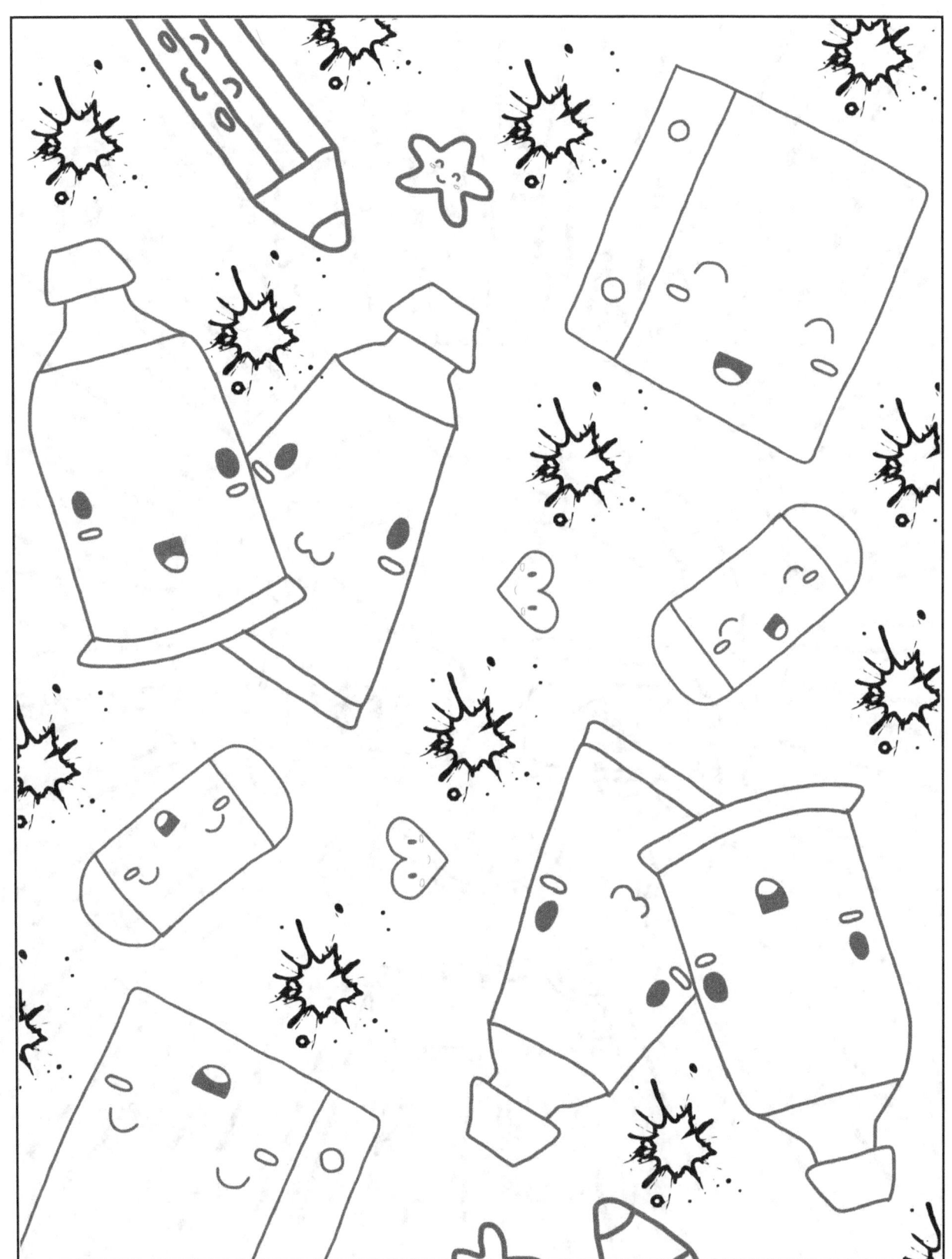

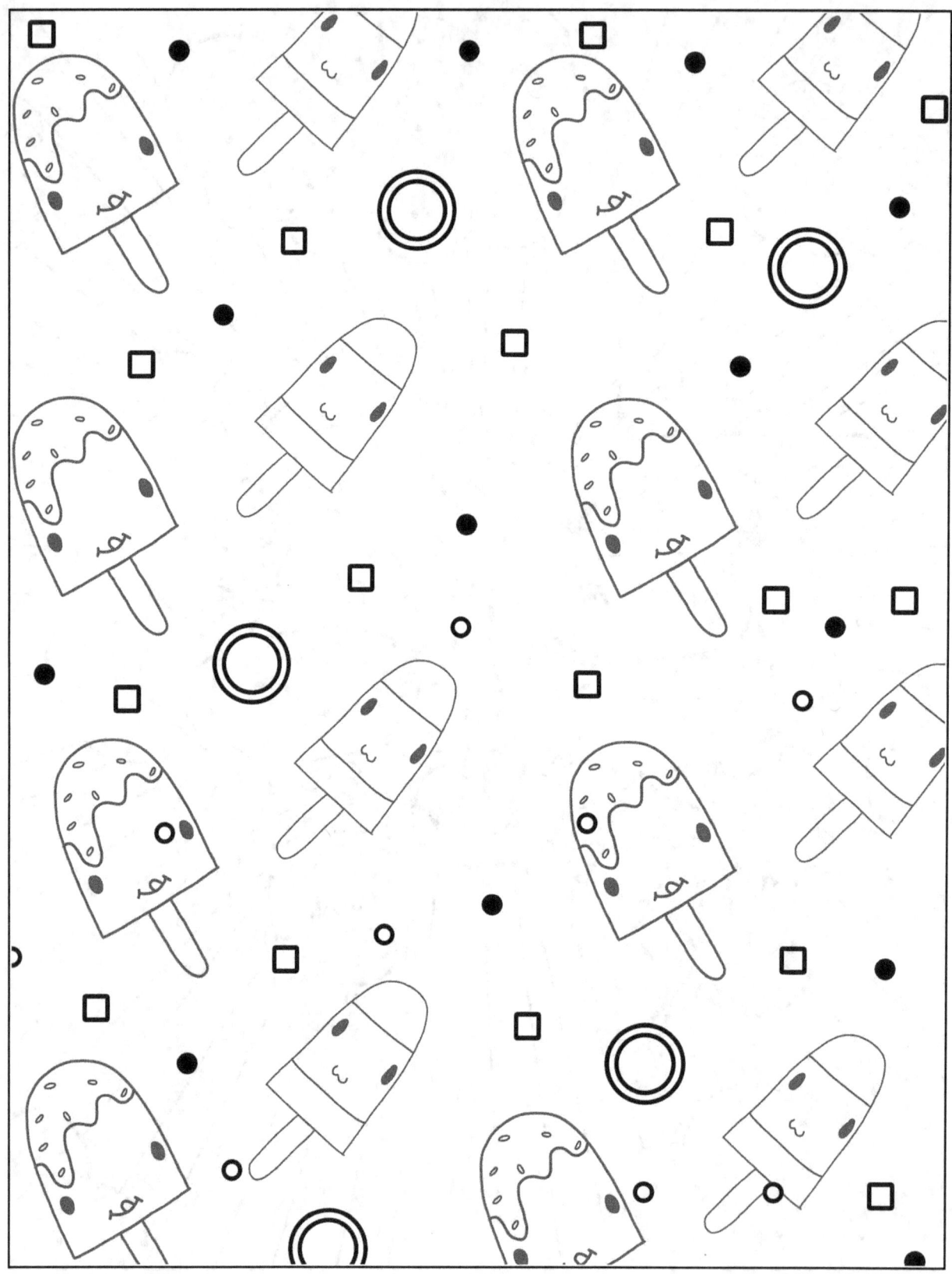

www.ingramcontent.com/pod-product-compliance
Lightning Source LLC
Chambersburg PA
CBHW081813280526
45789CB00008B/3113